MODEL CITY

Also by Donna Stonecipher

Poetry
The Reservoir
Souvenir de Constantinople
The Cosmopolitan

Translation
Ascent by Ludwig Hohl

Donna Stonecipher

MODEL CITY

Shearsman Books

First published in the United Kingdom in 2015 by
Shearsman Books
50 Westons Hill Drive
Emersons Green
BRISTOL BS16 7DF

Shearsman Books Ltd Registered Office
30-31 St. James Place, Mangotsfield, Bristol BS16 9JB
(this address not for correspondence)

www.shearsman.com

ISBN 978-1-84861-388-1

Copyright © Donna Stonecipher, 2015.

The right of Donna Stonecipher to be identified as the author of this work has been asserted by her in accordance with the Copyrights, Designs and Patents Act of 1988. All rights reserved.

ACKNOWLEDGMENTS
may be found on pages 91-92.

MODEL CITY

"We are waiting for a form of town planning that will give us freedom."
— Le Corbusier

Q:

What was it like?

Model City [1]

It was like slowly becoming aware one winter that there are new buildings going up all over your city, and then realizing that every single one of them is a hotel.

*

It was like thinking about all those empty rooms at night, all those empty rooms being built to hold an absence, as you lie in your bed at night, unable to sleep.

*

It was like the feeling of falling through the 'o' in 'hotel' as you almost fall asleep in your own bed, the bed that you own, caught at the last minute by ownership, the ownership of your wide-awake self.

*

It was like giving in to your ownership of yourself and going to the window, looking out at all the softly illuminated versions of the word 'hotel' announcing their shifting absences all over the city.

Model City [2]

It was like driving out of your way to visit a model city built next to an iron ore mine, a paragon of city planning, its well-spaced streetlamps casting small cones of light upon the darknesses of human life.

*

It was like arriving in the mostly abandoned model city and being unable to discern the features that make it a model city, for all its features have been incorporated into other cities, because they were so model.

*

It was like driving down the boarded-up main street of the model city with your windows down, and suspecting that you have come to the wrong model city, that the new model city, the right model city, lies far off.

*

It was like standing in a cone of light cast by one of the well-spaced streetlamps of the wrong model city, mined of all its ideas, its boarded-up windows hiding long-forgotten aspirations for a model life.

Model City [3]

It was like passing by a small shop under an overpass one afternoon in an unfamiliar part of a familiar city, and noticing that every single article for sale in it is blue.

*

It was like stopping in one's tracks outside the shop of blue articles and leaning in to gaze closer through the window, over part of which is reflected the blue sky.

*

It was like gazing transfixed at the blue articles, at the sky-blue, royal-blue, forget-me-not blue pencil sets and T-shirts, hairbrushes and egg cups, detaching themselves from the reflection of blue sky.

*

It was like knowing that you would never have passed by the shop in the familiar part of the city, and that familiarity with the blue shop will only make this part of the city even more — perpetually — unfamiliar.

Model City [4]

It was like seeing a fox one day right in the middle of the city — a real fox, not a taxidermied fox, nor a fox logo, nor a foxy person that one might want to sleep with.

*

It was like stopping and staring at the fox, along with all the other people walking down the street, all stopped in their tracks and staring in astonishment at the fox.

*

It was like watching the real, soft, cinnamon-colored fox, the only object moving in the landscape, moving silkily along the overgrown median, darting glances over at the people standing on the sidewalk, staring.

*

It was like the concentrated attention placed on the fox's perplexing appearance deflected by the fox, who keeps moving down the street, headed to a fox den known only to the fox — dark, liquid, solvent.

Model City [5]

It was like riding in a taxi through the streets of a foreign city and finding your gaze drawn to the 'Zu vermieten' signs in the tall windows of the Belle Epoque buildings.

*

It was like imagining renting an apartment in one of the Belle Epoque buildings and thereafter belonging to the foreign city, no longer foreign yourself, looking out your tall windows at foreigners riding by in taxis.

*

It was like thinking about the psychological space of the rental, taxi-like, offering a blank segment of the city in which to unfold your own foreignnesses and domesticities, about the hard beauty of the rental contract.

*

It was like looking at the 'Zu vermieten' signs and thinking about the organizing principle of the window: organizing light and air, inside and outside, volume and surplus, belonging and not belonging, opaque as glass.

Model City [6]

It was like the Socialist dream of the palace of culture, to place all culture in one marble building in the center of the city, like a big marble filing cabinet in which to file culture away.

*

It was like requisitioning the idea of the palace and bequeathing it to the people, who would come and become kings and queens in the royaume of the filing cabinet of culture.

*

It was like entering the palace of culture and walking down the endless yellow marble hallways leading to rooms, lecture halls, stages for culture — and feeling filed away oneself, a curious tourist queen.

*

It was like the dream of writing poems lined with endless yellow marble hallways, interrupted from time to time by the crystal orgasms of chandeliers, it was like the desire to write in Socialist Baroque.

Model City [7]

It was like bringing a picnic lunch with friends one Sunday to a converted industrial park, built over a closed mine, or an old quarry filled with lakewater, repurposed.

*

It was like setting out the grapes and the French cheese and the wine on the blue checked tablecloth, spread over the innocuous-seeming earth, seeded with secrets.

*

It was like suddenly, green grape in mouth, understanding the tenacity of landscape to seem, and your own tenacity to the seemliness of the landscape, to the rigor of the picnic.

*

It was like swimming after the picnic in the man-made lake flooding the quarry, dynamite blasts as rumored as the stocked fish nibbling speculatively at your ankles.

Model City [8]

It was like coming out of an unfamiliar subway station headed for a destination and noticing a sign that says 'Sugar Museum, 500 m' and suddenly changing your plans for the day, your destination.

*

It was like walking along the '500 m' announced by the sign for the Sugar Museum and thinking, only 500 m to the unending sweetness I deserve, your original destination forgotten under a cascade of sugar crystals.

*

It was like riding dutifully on the subway to a destination and knowing nothing of the Sugar Museum, knowing only destination, knowing nothing of the Sugar Museum and how it can alter plans.

*

It was like walking 200 m and then suddenly understanding the nature of the Sugar Museum, and turning around to set out again for your original destination. For its nature is seduction. And yours, renunciation.

Model City [9]

It was like walking down a street walked down many times before in your own neighborhood, and coming to a stop before a wide-open door that is usually never open.

*

It was like hesitating, and then walking through the open door into a courtyard, through which can be glimpsed another courtyard, through which can be glimpsed still another.

*

It was like walking through each glimpsed courtyard and glimpsing more courtyards, and walking through more and more glimpsed courtyards until you abruptly reach the last courtyard.

*

It was like staring at the last courtyard, its walls fluttering with red leaves like red sequins, and then turning forcefully around to glimpse all the courtyards in reverse, forcing them all to once again lie before you.

Model City [10]

It was like reading *The Arcades Project* and thinking about how grand it would be to go shopping in the past, when every store was an antiques store, and any antique could be had for a song.

*

It was like reading *The Arcades Project* and thinking about how time adds or subtracts value to objects and people, how some objects come to us like savants out of the past, embossed with knowledge.

*

It was like putting down *The Arcades Project*, switching off the light and lying in the dark badly wanting a first edition of *Les Fleurs du Mal*, badly wanting an original Atget.

*

It was like lying in the dark wondering if one would have known back then what one knows now, or if one can recognize value only after history recognizes it, if one merely apes the intelligence of time.

Model City [11]

It was like walking past the brown façade of a squat that has been evacuated by force and gutted, on which is still painted in large white letters WIR BLEIBEN ALLE.

*

It was like stopping to look at the façade and its gaping black window slots, behind which no one at all remains, and trying to decide if it is a good or a bad thing that you don't have your camera.

*

It was like trying to decide if taking a photograph of the gutted squat would be ethical or unethical, if, in taking a photograph, you would be like Weegee photographing a corpse, or Audubon painting a dead bluebird.

*

It was like moving on past the gutted squat and its gutted ideal: to live without money in a 21st-century European late capitalist capital city, knowing thousands of other cameras will take the photograph that you do not.

Model City [12]

It was like wandering through an ersatz medieval town and wondering how many centuries it would take to turn into a real town, or even if it ever could, since its origins were ersatz.

*

It was like marveling at the precision of detail in the ersatz town, its illuminations and crenellations, and also at the mistakes, the well-meaning mistakes in execution, in executing the real ersatz.

*

It was like wondering about the viability of the ersatz medieval town, peopled only by tourists and stocked with expensive ersatz Heimat cafés — just like real medieval towns all over the continent.

*

It was like wandering through the ersatz town and wondering about the origin of ersatz, about the authenticity of authenticity, about the sorrows of patina, the magnificent duplicities of age.

Model City [13]

It was like traveling to visit a model city and finding yourself in a museum looking at architectural models of the model city, set atop pedestals like reliquaries containing the human need to idealize.

*

It was like realizing after a time that you are lingering among the model city models because they contain idealization like reliquaries, as the model city itself cannot, and what you have come to the model city for is idealization.

*

It was like traveling to the model city for idealization and realizing you have found it in the models of the model city, in which idealization, safe from space and time, can't fall into ruin.

*

It was like imagining yourself as a figure in one of the models frozen in the act of crossing the model city's plaza, frozen forever in your need to idealize in the midst of a realized ideal.

Model City [14]

It was like walking past a person taking photographs of a white Bauhaus building and suddenly deciding to enter the building, to insist on an interior in the face of the photographer's insistence on façade.

*

It was like entering the Bauhaus building which was like breaking into the façade which was like leaping into a dark pond in which a white Bauhaus building is reflected with photographic precision, shattering the reflection.

*

It was like feeling contempt for the photographer reducing the white Bauhaus building via his camera to form without content, line without space — privileging façade.

*

It was like allowing yourself a moment of triumph upon shattering the building's façade and insisting on its interiority, as you briefly become part of the building — a kind of column or a soffit.

Model City [15]

It was like reading in a math book about the 'Droste effect,' a mathematician's term for infinite regress, and remembering the old Droste cocoa tin you once owned and loved when you lived in another city.

*

It was like reading further that the 'Droste effect,' term of mathematicians, was named after the old red Droste cocoa tins like the one you once loved and nevertheless gave away when you left another city.

*

It was like remembering how the nurse holding a tray of cocoa on the tin was depicted in the tin on her tray, in which she held a tray with a tin depicting her holding a tray with a tin depicting her holding a tray with a tin, and so on.

*

It was like wanting to plunge through the infinite regress of nurses holding trays of cocoa down to the tiniest nurse's tray, where you will find the tin that you once gave away when you had to leave another city you loved.

Model City [16]

It was like going to an exhibition where all the artworks are about melancholy, and falling into fits of uncontrollable laughter, especially before a case of little ivory skeletons "intended for private reflection."

*

It was like looking at the faces on those skeletons and asking yourself why skulls are always grinning like that, what they have to grin about, and then realizing we are all always grinning like that, under our faces.

*

It was like feeling that grin under your face at all times, even when you are sobbing, or expressionless, reading a thick book late at night next to a dark window: there you are grinning, despite yourself, down at the book.

*

It was like leaving the melancholy exhibition nearly sobbing with laughter, picturing the memento mori, the tiny skeletons in some noblewoman's gloved hand, as she privately reflects, secretly grinning.

Model City [17]

It was like watching the city slowly powdered over with snow from your bedroom window, the molecular makeup of the city slowly altered through powdery intimations of ossification.

*

It was like watching the snow slowly powder over the construction site across the street, which will one day be a hotel, the snow filling in the space temporarily where one day there will be permanent temporariness.

*

It was like slowly coming to think of the snow as permanent, the construction site as permanent, the grand opening of the hotel permanently postponed, the spring postponed, the grand opening of the crocuses.

*

It was like feeling powdered over with snow oneself, as one is part of the city; apart from it, watching it from the window, to be sure; but a part of it, a powdered-over temporary part.

Model City [18]

It was like traveling to see the Alhambra and ending up spending most of the day in the Alhambra archive, leafing through books, studying photographs, and watching films about the Alhambra.

*

It was like feeling very guilty but also very calm in the archive, feeling the bright calm of mediation, daydreaming over the black-and-white Persian gardens in a film, the Palace of the Nasrid in a brown ink drawing.

*

It was like willing the bright calm of mediation to delete your guilt as you hold a book of sepia photographs and place your hand over the stylized hand of Fatima carved into a stone portal.

*

It was like wishing you could walk outside and find the entire Alhambra tinted sepia, because you'd feel so much calmer in a sepia Alhambra than in the real Alhambra, with its real greenery so green, so real.

Model City [19]

It was like reading in *Towards a New Architecture* of Le Corbusier's veneration of the white paint, rows of windows, and spiral staircases of transatlantic ships: a "pure, clean, bright, correct, and healthy architecture."

*

It was like venerating Le Corbusier's veneration of the austere architecture of transatlantic ships while your mind drifts off to more of a Victorian interior: niches and secret stairways, eaves, chinoiserie screens, ormolu.

*

It was like admiring and resisting the machine for living, aspirations toward the shipshape, faces neatly framed in portholes, bodies in tennis whites leaning on the ship railing of reason.

*

It was like wanting to divide your two-room apartment into the Le Corbusien and the Victorian, one room "correct and healthy," one room diseased and false, sailing to nowhere but its own green-velvet unreason.

Model City [20]

It was like giving a tour of your city to a history professor and suddenly forgetting the history of every building, every monument, every landmark you pass, in quick succession.

*

It was like fumbling outwardly to explain to the nice history professor that you knew these histories once, but knowing inwardly that facts have little traction in your mind.

*

It was like walking along with the history professor trying to remember which era the professor researches, which war the movie on the marquee presages, in which century the church before you was built, what year it is.

*

It was like wishing you could explain to the history professor how the city resides in your head: like a well-worn atlas of beauties and shocks, not a-historical, but not ordered by history; actual, but not necessarily factual.

Model City [21]

It was like looking out at the city's motley collection of random skyscrapers from various eras and wondering if they signified the energy and vigor of democracy, or its venal ennui.

*

It was like looking at the skyscrapers' staggered heights on the horizon and wondering if somebody somewhere had thought that this homage to a ridgeline would ameliorate the lack of the sublime in city life.

*

It was like looking out at the skyscrapers' staggering heights and motley randomness and then wondering if there could even be such a thing as a democratic sublime.

*

It was like the young architect sitting at her window looking out for hours at the city skyline and making lists of which buildings are beautiful and which are sublime.

Model City [22]

It was like walking through the perfume department of a department store in your adopted city and smelling exactly the same perfume-clouds as those that hover in department stores in your native city.

*

It was like walking through the perfume-clouds and feeling both attracted and repulsed, as the sickeningly sweet perfume-clouds first cushion, then suffocate you with thoughts of home.

*

It was like walking past the row of smiling women in white coats proffering perfume samples amid the discreet hush of commerce, which is exactly the same discreet hush in your native and in the foreign city.

*

It was like breathing in the perfume-clouds of commerce amid the store's discreet pervasive hush, wishing you could distinguish the synthetic musk from the real musk, the real myrrh.

Model City [23]

It was like studying plans for a concentric model city consisting of rings of houses and gardens, factories, markets, a crystal palace, a "farm for epileptics," and a "home for inebriates."

*

It was like looking at a close-up of the concentric rings in which life is to be parceled out, ordered, rendered spatially lucid, and noticing, behind the circular railway, an allocation for a jam factory.

*

It was like imagining strawberry and raspberry jam circulating neutrally among the theoretical inhabitants of the model city, jam for breakfast in the gardens of the well-to-do and at the epileptic farm.

*

It was like wondering what would happen if the inebriates were to choose not to remain spatially lucid in their allotted parcel of land, if the jam were to burst out of the factory vats and cover the model city in sweet red salve.

Model City [24]

It was like standing in the midst of a city park with a friend who shows you that if you stare too long at the artificial waterfall, then look away, the waterfall will suddenly start to rush not down, but up.

*

It was like discovering how to make the waterfall rush in reverse and then standing there making it happen over and over, staring too long at the waterfall rushing down, then rushed back up by your will.

*

It was like willing the artificial waterfall to rush back up in the midst of the city park in the midst of the city, crisscrossed with concrete fences constructed to look like wood, all constructed of will.

*

It was like dreaming that night of the waterfall in winter, surrounded by silver skyscrapers, halted by cold in its downward rush, a torrent of icicles, neither rushing up nor rushing down, impervious to will.

Model City [25]

It was like walking home from a movie theater with your loved one, unable to stop singing "Wie einst, Lili Marleen..." "Wie einst, Lili Marleen..." when you pass a poster with blue lettering for an exhibit on the *città ideale*.

*

It was like going back home to your small apartment and remembering having read somewhere that Leonardo da Vinci wrote somewhere that small rooms strengthen minds, while large rooms weaken them.

*

It was like turning on the television and idly sketching a new *città ideale*, one in which all the rooms are so tiny that minds swell in them like da Vinci heads in drawings — large, correct, teeming with inventions.

*

It was like making sure to draw at least one window into each room, so that nowhere in the *città ideale* could a person be put into a windowless room to be tortured by endless iterations of "Lili Marleen."

Model City [26]

It was like hearing about a neighborhood on the outskirts of your adopted city called the 'Cosmos Quarter,' lined with streets with names like Venus and Sirius.

*

It was like forming the plan to take the subway out to the Cosmos Quarter one Saturday, and then hearing that in recent years the quarter has fallen into a depressed state, a piece of news you listen to with delight.

*

It was like taking delight in the cleft between the universe of optimism that could name the streets of the Cosmos Quarter Venus and Sirius, and the depressed state into which the quarter has fallen like a burnt-out comet.

*

It was like, later, wondering at your easy ability to abstract suffering into the picturesque, then wondering what wondrous effect you had expected anyway in the Cosmos Quarter, in reading its outworn semiotics of zeal.

Model City [27]

It was like driving around a model city in which each house is required to have a porch and forbidden to have a lawn, and thinking about the loveliness of lawns, the sound of lawn-mowers out of childhood.

*

It was like driving around the lawn-less model city, so friendly with its porches, and thinking about how its friendliness is held in place by control, like a drawing held in place by fixative, so the charcoal won't smudge.

*

It was like driving around the friendly model city held in position only by laws and decrees, by writs and punishments and threats of expulsion, and thinking about the lovely irresponsibility of lawns.

*

It was like looking upon the lawnless model city and wishing one could live there *but also* have a lawn, a porch *and* a lawn — lush with dew at dawn, dark velvet at nightfall, as the lawn-mowers are going home.

Model City [28]

It was like going to see "The Unbuilt City," an exhibition of plans and models designed to transform your city — grids, towers, monumental ministries, vast plazas — that came to nothing.

*

It was like wandering through the exhibit looking at futuristic drawings that erase the past, the nineteenth-century four-story architecture you love, and feeling supremely pleased the plans came to nothing.

*

It was like taking note of a resistance in yourself to the futuristic, the futuresque, the future — while not denying a certain nostalgia for antiquated visions of the world of tomorrow.

*

It was like looking at the futuristic models and thinking about the unbearableness of the present, and realizing there are two kinds of people: those who can't wait for the future, and those who can't wait for the past.

Model City [29]

It was like taking digital photograph after digital photograph of lilac bushes in the city park, moving with your digital camera right into the lilac bushes, because you are in love and out of your mind.

*

It was like filling up your digital camera's memory with bad photographs of lilacs and only lilacs, lilacs blowzily expanding to fill the four corners of all the frames.

*

It was like walking right into the lilac bushes with your digital camera like a person hypnotized, pressing the button again and again to memorize the blowzy lilacs, to digitize the out-of-your-mindness of being in love.

*

It was like being in love and out of your mind and walking straight into the lilac bushes to take bad digital photographs of the lilacs — though you know it won't be long before you sit, bemused, deleting each one.

Model City [30]

It was like trying to find a café that was not a Starbucks or Balzac or Einstein in an unknown city known for its coffeehouses, and finally giving up and ordering a tall skinny latte with the familiar chaste mermaid on the cup.

*

It was like resuming your walk through the unknown city holding a cup of global capital, your familiar chaste mermaid added to the thousands of chaste mermaids parading through the city.

*

It was like wondering if any writers or scientists are sitting in Starbucks or Balzac or Einstein adding to the world's storehouse of knowledge as they sip fair-trade dark-roasted liquid global capital in cups with chaste mermaids.

*

It was like reminding yourself to add *Moby-Dick* to your Amazon shopping cart, and then passing a small bookstore with a sign in the window in the unknown language (it says: LIQUIDATION SALE: EVERYTHING MUST GO).

Model City [31]

It was like walking one evening through the violent anachronisms and disused clocktowers of a city that had once tried and failed to impede the march of time, and finding yourself invaded by a feeling.

*

It was like taking in the vanquished clocktowers and further markers of the vanquishing march of time as you realize that the feeling is nostalgia — for a past not your own, all the more potent for its double displacement.

*

It was like slowing your pace before a fortress and coming to a stop, stopping to mark this moment in time, in recognition of the desire to stop it, it was like halting the march of your own borrowed nostalgia, trying to vanquish it.

*

It was like accidentally glancing down at your watch, then accidentally up at the clocktower, and feeling the double vanquishing of time, the stoppage and the ticking — the ticking, the ticking.

Model City [32]

It was like taking a taxi out of the city to go to the beach with friends one Sunday, to lie almost comatose with pleasure, to melt into the sky and to lie on the sand like a sand dollar with no possessions.

*

It was like arriving at the beach, paying the taxi driver, listening to the waves, and then noticing the profusion of shells washed up in ridged rows on the beach, the sea's depository.

*

It was like lying on the sand almost comatose with pleasure for an hour or so, and then finding yourself drawn to the ridged rows of the shells, their articulated forms, their coin-like precision.

*

It was like spending the rest of the day collecting shells and only later, adding them to your possessions, remembering you had gone to the beach to melt into the sky, to lie comatose with pleasure like a sand dollar on the sand.

Model City [33]

It was like listening to a citizen of a country that no longer exists talk about how he was forced to choose a new country, and how he chose for his new country a language — a foreign language.

*

It was like hearing about how he chose a foreign language and set about to build a home in it, perfecting its accent and then disappearing into its glottals and labials — for a home is by definition disappearance.

*

It was like thinking about missing disappearing into your own country, and wondering if a foreign language can also offer disappearance. He, the citizen, knows home is a construction.

*

It was like the citizen knowing that home is a construction exposing our own constructedness; he chose the most beautiful foreign language and tried to disappear into its declinations.

Model City [34]

It was like watching swallows crisscross over the plazas of the Alhambra and thinking of the expression "bird's-eye view," and wondering aloud if the swallows are enjoying the view.

*

It was like watching the swallows crisscross over the springtime Alhambra while posing an absurd question aloud to the person with whom one has just shared a first kiss in a hotel.

*

It was like imagining all the bird's-eye views enjoyed by all the birds crisscrossing the Alhambra, the swallows threading in and out of the towers and the fortress, whose entrance is carefully hidden.

*

It was like walking in the Alhambra enjoying feeling absurd and desirous, posing absurd questions and kissing the person no longer in the hotel — which welcomes anyone — but next to the fortress, which welcomes no one.

Model City [35]

It was like noticing hotel after hotel going up all over the city with unstoppable force and imagining a city consisting only of hotels, a city composed solely of expensive emptinesses.

*

It was like remembering that you had rented the apartment you live in exactly because it felt like a hotel room, radiating a friendly indifference, because it felt like the right measure of you to your life.

*

It was like thinking about the nights you walked through the city feeling threatened by the rampantly multiplying hotel rooms, as if vacancy were a disease invading the city's — and therefore your — interior.

*

It was like wondering if the city has an interior, and if so exactly how much it costs, it was like wanting to add up all the prices for the hotel rooms and all the rents in the city to find out exactly how much the city's interior costs.

Model City [37]

It was like walking through an industrial model city to get to fields of blue forget-me-nots beyond it, fields that no one planted, where blue forget-me-nots spring up sweetly and industrially.

*

It was like wanting to forget everything, but remembering to stoop down to pick a forget-me-not to place in your notebook, its pages monumental and blank, where the blue forget-me-not will desiccate into a sign.

*

It was like remembering that no one planned or planted the forget-me-nots as you lie intoxicated among them, their tiny blue faces both curious and blank, as you forget your own industrial curiosity.

*

It was like putting your coat back on and leaving the field of forget-me-nots, everything you'd hoped not to remember springing back into your mind as you forget your notebook with the forget-me-not in the unplanned field.

Model City [38]

It was like hearing an architect talk about standing at the ocean studying the structure of the waves, the ornament of the seafoam, construction and destruction, construction and deconstruction.

*

It was like hearing the architect say he'd thought about the wave insisting on its own ridged architectonics, on the dialectics of building solutions and dissolutions, on liquid *Baukunst*, as he espied spiral seashells in the sand.

*

It was like the architect saying he'd like to build rooms in which the sleeper falls asleep to the sound of the waves, a sound like overlapping stadia filling and emptying, a bedroom like a spiraled seashell.

*

It was like listening to the architect say he wanted to construct the rooms out of the sound of the waves, and wanting to fall asleep curved into the structure of the spiraled seashell, ushered to sleep by dissolving waves.

Model City [39]

It was like walking through the city one evening and suddenly noticing all of the advertisements advertising advertisement: Rent this space for X amount per day.

*

It was like never having noticed before how much of the city's advertising space was advertising itself, and stopping to wind your scarf more tightly around your neck.

*

It was like feeling unable to fend off the chilly mise-en-abyme of the advertisements advertising themselves, as if you had accidentally placed a fingertip on the city's tender spot.

*

It was like turning direction for home to get away from the unsightly sight of the city advertising itself, offering up all its blank surfaces for purchase — worse, for rental.

Model City [40]

It was like going to visit a summer palace built for a queen and later requisitioned by socialists, restored and opened to the public as a museum — with socialist-royalist gift shop.

*

It was like walking into the former drawing room turned into the socialists' council chamber, the massive drab-green furniture arranged under the queen's gilded mirrors, which the socialists left on the walls.

*

It was like noticing that the socialists left the bourgeois gilded filigree mirrors on the walls, and reading on the wall panel that the socialists' drab green furniture had cost "a small fortune."

*

It was like lingering in a blue bedroom that had once hosted the dreams of princes, and then the dreams of Castro, Qaddafi, Gorbachev, Ceaușescu … and feeling a frisson about what souvenirs you might find in the gift shop.

Model City [41]

It was like seeing a little group of American tourists in a European city tremble with excitement when the tour guide points out bullet holes from World War II still visible in the parliament building.

*

It was like the group of tourists nodding politely at the new glass buildings, dutifully admiring the skillfully renovated museums they walk by, but only trembling to life before the building pocked with bullet holes.

*

It was like the little group of American tourists stopping and trembling with excitement at the holes, trembling at this unexpected apparition of evidence — that history is real.

*

It was like watching one of the tourists go right up to a bullet hole and stick his finger into it — to the envious gasps of the rest of the tourists, who want to feel real bullets rip through their own peacetime lives.

Model City [42]

It was like standing on the street watching a delivery truck drive down into an underground parking garage, watching it get smaller and smaller until it looks like a toy truck before it disappears.

*

It was like watching the delivery truck drive deep down into the garage and then disappear into the darkness as the automatic gate at street level slowly lowers to the ground.

*

It was like thinking that night about the underground parking garage and all the other underground garages in the city constructing a city as deep under the ground as the high-rises construct a city high over the city.

*

It was like smoking a cigarette in one's high-rise thinking about the three cities, each glittering with its own gravitational attraction, and then about the deliveries disappearing into the underground city.

Model City [43]

It was like sitting on the sofa reading a book about a model city in which the building code decrees all windows must be vertical; in this model city, no horizontal windows are allowed.

*

It was like reading the explanation in the book that vertical windows "reflect a standing person" and wondering why windows that "reflect a sitting person" would not be allowed.

*

It was like thinking about the significance of standing vs. the significance of sitting, the ethics of the vertical vs. the horizontal, the bad morality of the picture window, dissolute in horizontality.

*

It was like putting down the book and looking out one's own horizontal picture window, through which one voyeurizes one's neighbors — making a picture of the neighborhood, but not allowing oneself to be in it.

Model City [44]

It was like standing in the supermarket in front of rows and rows of Swiss chocolate bars, all of whose wrappers are printed with either paintings or photographs of snow-covered Alps.

*

It was like noticing that the Swiss chocolate bars with paintings of snow-covered Alps on their wrappers are more expensive than the chocolate bars with photographs of snow-covered Alps.

*

It was like reflecting that the paintings of the snow-covered Alps on the chocolate bars are also, after all, photographs, and smiling to yourself at the persistence of the market value of the mystique of the singular.

*

It was like hesitating, then picturing the massive vats of chocolate out of which each singular bar has been molded, then picking out one with a painting of snow-covered Alps on it — because you, after all, are also singular.

Model City [45]

It was like going out to look for a bank in your new neighborhood and noticing a store called the Umsonst Laden — the "free store," where nothing costs anything — stacked with piles of dusty books.

*

It was like feeling nervous each time you walk past the Umsonst Laden to get to your bank, wondering if, the next time you walk by, the Umsonst Laden will even still be there.

*

It was like, one day, turning the corner onto the street of the Umsonst Laden and hesitating, then turning back to go down another street to get to your bank, because the Umsonst Laden makes you too nervous.

*

It was like a year later accidentally walking again down the street of the Umsonst Laden and seeing a hole where it had been, and sighing: the torment of idealism is over, the street may now return to the real.

Model City [46]

It was like reading in the newspaper one morning that the city's building minister has placed a moratorium on the construction of new hotels, and feeling yourself flooded with relief.

*

It was like only at that moment realizing how the proliferation of new hotels has filled your own head with vacancies, how each new hotel has added 50, 100, 200 emptinesses to a proliferation of emptinesses.

*

It was like suddenly thinking about the emptinesses in yourself: your body with its cells, your heart with its chambers. There were already too many emptinesses.

*

It was like feeling your cells and chambers flooded with relief, though you sense that the moratorium may have come too late, that the city with all its hotels may have already slid irrevocably into vacancy.

Model City [47]

It was like watching the implosion of a damaged church captured on film, watching the brown façade implode, slide down, the steeple tip to the side and sink down into the unbuilt in a film.

*

It was like watching the built slide ecstatically into the unbuilt in a film, and feeling it, as you watch, as voluptuous but violent, a violent voluptuousness sliding past the tension of the built.

*

It was like watching the tension of maintaining walls and floors, of keeping the steeple erect, give in to the ecstasy of implosion, of letting the steeple slide weightlessly down into the brown billowing dust-clouds of the unbuilt.

*

It was like watching the church implode in the film and feeling ecstatic and voluptuous oneself, wanting to press "rewind" to watch the implosion over and over, its slide into voluptuousness, its fuck-you to the built.

Model City [48]

It was like sitting by the sea with an architect friend in Barcelona chairs looking out at the panorama of relentlessness that is the horizon line, allowing its absolution to enter your body.

*

It was like feeling your body tense up as you stare at the panorama of the horizon line, the edge where the sea meets the sky and there is no compromise, an edge facing off an edge.

*

It was like feeling this panoramic edge of the horizon line where there is no compromise in your body in its Barcelona chair as a kind of vertigo, and briefly lowering your head.

*

It was like looking up again and wishing you could hire your architect-friend to cover the ocean with towers and spires to block out the panoramic horizon line and its absolute absolutism.

Model City [49]

It was like taking the train across a border between two countries with disparate languages, one built like a fortress and one slinky as a river, and thinking about how orderly languages are, keeping within their borders.

*

It was like anticipating how the station-names will change abruptly from words stout as fortresses to words slinky as rivers right after the border, as if each language lived in a world untroubled by the existence of the other.

*

It was like crossing the border and trying to feel it underneath the train, to feel this instance of division, of order, of force, of fate. But the border was an abstraction ordering other abstractions, like stout and slinky languages.

*

It was like noticing the train has stopped at the border and seeing a woman outside with the wrong passport apprehended by police — and remembering the luxury of forgetting the brute ordering force of abstractions.

Model City [50]

It was like walking past a building that had been built by one regime and then used by three regimes in succession, and thinking about the idea of ownership, of a building as an exoskeleton of a regime.

*

It was like thinking about the building that you call home as an exoskeleton you do not in any sense own, unlike a snail's exoskeleton; about the ownership of attachment, the attachment to ownership.

*

It was like remembering pulling empty snail-shells from wildflower leaves one summer, and remembering that even snails don't own their own homes, that one doesn't even own one's own skeleton.

*

It was like straightening up your borrowed skeleton while entering the exoskeleton of the building, knowing that you are only a regime moving into the abandoned homes of previous regimes.

Model City [51]

It was like moving into an apartment for the summer furnished only with a bed, a desk, a chair, and an old "world" radio in a brown case, its luminous dial turning to Moscow Berlin Paris Skopje Budapest London and Tangier.

*

It was like lying in bed at night next to the world-radio, etched with distant cities, which now only gets local stations, and imagining lying in bed in Skopje in the last century listening to music from Paris.

*

It was like lying under the open window thinking the apartment is not big enough, the summer is not big enough, the world is not big enough for the world-radio with its etched cities and its luminous ideals.

*

It was like leaving the apartment at summer's end and sneaking the world-radio out in your suitcase, for you know that only you understand the radio's faith in a grander, more worldly world — and its inability to transmit it.

Model City [52]

It was like passing a public flowerbed on your way to work and noticing the tulips have been torn out to make way for violets, which will be torn out to make way for pansies, which will be torn out to make way for forget-me-nots.

*

It was like thinking about all those torn-out flowers lying in heaps on wheelbarrows to be carted away for the sake of the beautiful illusion of perpetual bloom, about sacrifice and waste, meaningless labor and graft.

*

It was like sitting at home after work thinking of one's own meaningless labor, of all the money spent on public gardens, of this social contract upon the meaning of beauty, one of the few on which the many agree.

*

It was like thinking about all those torn-out tulips and violets, pansies and forget-me-nots, lying in meaningless heaps on wheelbarrows, the irrationality of an economy of beauty, the flower-like ecstasy of the irrational.

Model City [53]

It was like taking a taxi one night through the streets of your adopted city to get home to your rented apartment, and passing new hotel after new hotel in every neighborhood.

*

It was like seeing the word HOTEL echoing through the city and feeling the urge to take off your clothes in the taxi, and then to see how much if any of your skin you can take off, to get down to some thing you own.

*

It was like wanting to take off everything, clothes, skin, down to the heart working inside your body, and thinking about how our bodies are hotels for guests we may know but have never seen.

*

It was like arriving home and entering your rented apartment like the hotel guest that you are at heart, knowing that you own nothing, not even the vacant body you offer to your loved one.

Model City [54]

It was like realizing in the Alhambra that you are having a beautiful experience that is not infinite, and trying to snatch something of it, to defy the laws of space and time.

*

It was like having a beautiful experience in the Alhambra and seeing yourself as in a glass case as you look at yourself having the experience, encased in glass and unable to snatch anything of it.

*

It was like being in a glass case in the Alhambra being watched by yourself, and seeing your face reflected in the glass, your finite face avid with desire to snatch something of it.

*

It was like wanting to smash the glass case so that you can at least snatch a shard of glass with which to pierce the beautiful finite experience, pierce it to infinity.

Model City [55]

It was like going to another part of the city to visit an apartment complex built over the autobahn, and imagining what it would be like to live in that building suspended over speed.

*

It was like thinking about this confluence of motion and stillness, speed and rest, restlessness and home, and wondering what it would be like to sleep over such a display of awakeness.

*

It was like imagining making love to one's beloved in a bed bolted to the floor built over the foundations suspended above the steady roar of cars held to no speed limit.

*

It was like sitting on the floor in your own quiet apartment that night and wishing you could feel an autobahn running underneath it, an autobahn to inject your quiet home life with a cautionary roar.

Model City [56]

It was like dreaming that you are given the keys to a model city and feeling the burden of ownership, the keys weighing down your coat pocket so severely you start dreaming of giving them back.

*

It was like dreaming that you are given the keys to a model city and then you get into your royal blue car and drive out to the outskirts of town to leave the keys on an unoccupied bench overlooking a lake.

*

It was like dreaming that you drive back home unburdened, enter your house with its key and sit down with a sigh on your bed, in the quiet and dark, until you notice that the keys to the model city are back in your pocket.

*

It was like waking suddenly from the dream, seeing your house key on its hook, and luxuriating in the freedom from keys to model cities — in the deep ease of the haphazard and the habitual, the half-assed.

Model City [57]

It was like going to a dinner party in a foreign city and listening to the hostess talk about a cherry festival for which, the previous year, the organizers had had to import the cherries.

*

It was like considering the city faced with a cherry festival and no cherries, counting on the import's glossiness, its guileless slide into open mouths, on no one being able to tell the difference between native and foreign cherries.

*

It was like finding yourself envying the import, the ease with which goods made in one place are loaded onto airplanes, ships, and trucks and inserted glossily into other places.

*

It was like feeling a sudden urge to expose the festival exalting a harvest that never happened — *why should the import gloss over the native's failure?* you ask. And then cherry tarts were served.

Model City [58]

It was like walking through a Socialist model city that began life named for a dictator, that ten years later was hastily renamed for its industry, and that fifty years later than that is drastically shrinking.

*

It was like learning that the stiffly elegant Stalinist buildings in the center of the city were restored with government funds awarded for blowing up empty tower blocks on the outskirts.

*

It was like looking at the Stalinist buildings lining the city's streets — wide, honeyed with sunlight, utterly empty — and wishing you could have watched the tower blocks in its unseen outskirts blown to bits.

*

It was like seeing four violences in the partly blown-up renamed model city: 1. renaming 2. naming 3. destruction 4. creation. O we already know that to build means to lard with ideology — later regretted or no.

Model City [59]

It was like being an amateur photographer taking a boat tour through a city having forgotten your camera in the hotel, and feeling a bitter flash each time an aesthetic scene frames itself before your very eyes.

*

It was like seeing that each wasted aesthetic scene has a hidden significance suddenly revealed to you alone and just as suddenly vanishing, a bittersweet fleeting aesthetic scene.

*

It was like, the next day, setting out for the city with your camera and seeing not a single aesthetic scene framed for you alone, all day long — a long day — going back to the hotel with your film blank.

*

It was like sitting on the hotel bed and shoving your camera deep into your blue suitcase, resolving to go camera-less in the city from now on, preferring the nobility of your bitterness to the humiliations of blankness.

Model City [60]

It was like riding the bus to the airport on your way to fly home and catching a glimpse, through trees, of a parking lot covered with an endless expanse of cream-colored taxis.

*

It was like experiencing the moment as cinematic, how the bus rises slowly on its ramp, and the leafy trees part slowly and suggestively to reveal the endless expanse of cream-colored taxis.

*

It was like gazing down on the expanse of cream-colored taxis, then at the airport, then at the inside of the bus, with its permanent tableau of nervous travelers and precarious luggage sculptures.

*

It was like taking in the tableaux of permanent transitoriness and feeling yourself glide off the bus as if on a conveyer belt conveying you home — via bus and airplane, though you have a thing for cream-colored taxis.

Model City [61]

It was like arriving too early to visit the Freud Museum and being forced to walk around the neighborhood on a cold November morning, trying to blow heat into your hands.

*

It was like arriving too early, walking several times around the block, and wondering what psychopathology such earliness must reveal, especially for a person who is in her daily life chronically late.

*

It was like trying not to over-interpret this instance of earliness within a pattern of lateness while blowing meaninglessly into your hands, knowing the gesture must in fact be full of meaning.

*

It was like entering the house knowing your existence is a tangle of psychopathologies you will never unravel, and fixing your gaze on The Couch: so inviting with its velvet pillows, so roped off by velvet barriers.

Model City [62]

It was like walking through your neighborhood one snowy night with a new friend who'd lived there long ago, watching him point to long-gone restaurants and stores that used to make up the streetscape.

*

It was like feeling dismayed by this inscription of your new friend's perfected past all over the present, perfected and erased, except in the theater of his mind, all over the actual snowy streetscape, with its actual storefronts.

*

It was like trudging silently down the snowy street with the new friend pointing to long-gone storefronts, dismayed by the theater of the past drawing its blue velvet curtain over the present, as the snow erases both.

*

It was like sensing you won't see the new friend again, and realizing that every hour is a theater of victory or failure of the inscription of a present. You have just lived through an hour of failure, snowed under by the perfect past.

Model City [63]

It was like reading on the internet about a new opera house built in China by Zaha Hadid, and how it is beginning to crumble after having been open for only six months.

*

It was like thinking about the energy of architectural drawings and the exhaustion of standing, the exhaustion of the architect's perfect drawings being made to stand by the engineers.

*

It was like pitying the architect and faulting the engineers, admiring the engineers and envying the architect, placing the architect on a pedestal and not bothering to learn the names of the engineers.

*

It was like thinking about the energy of ideas and the exhaustion of realization, about the perfect opera house in Zaha Hadid's mind — which will take much longer to crumble.

Model City [64]

It was like going to the Secret Service museum and peering into vitrines displaying secret cameras — concealed in watches, purses, fountain pens, buttonholes, thermoses, neckties, and fake tree trunks.

*

It was like thinking about all the secret cameras hidden on agents peering into dark corners of the city gathering information like worker bees gathering pollen to deliver to the queen bee that is the state.

*

It was like thinking about the hive buzzing with worker bees eager to serve the queen bee of the state, and then discarding this metaphor from the natural world, because spies are spies, and bees are bees, and a state is a state.

*

It was like thinking about the camera hidden in the fake tree trunk, and then about the night you watched a deer peer into the living-room window of a suburban house, about the naturalness and unnaturalness of surveillance.

Model City [65]

It was like being driven through a neighborhood with no sidewalks in a small city and being told that sidewalks were intentionally not built so that "undesirable elements" could not walk too close to the houses.

*

It was like looking out the car window at the mid-century red-brick houses with their porches and white columns gliding by, presumably inhabited by "desirable elements."

*

It was like thinking about how cities conceal their secrets, which are nevertheless in plain view, as you notice that the white-columned porches going by are all empty.

*

It was like wondering how many other hidden desires are in plain view as you are driven away from the neighborhood with no sidewalks, its white columns toppled, one by one, in the rearview mirror.

Model City [66]

It was like strolling through a city with one's loved one down a street parked with SUVs and horse-and-carriages, and noticing a pair of yoked horses nuzzling while the driver, in a velveteen cape, waits for trade.

*

It was like reading affection into the velveteen nuzzling of the horses behind the SUVs and wondering, if one reads affection into the nuzzling of the yoked horses, is it affectionate?

*

It was like secretly wanting to take a ride in one of the carriages through the city, but instead decrying the plight of the yoked horses and scorning the shabbiness of velveteen anachronism.

*

It was like looking into the horses' brown velvet eyes and thinking about the horsepower of the SUVs, while walking down the street holding hands with one's loved one — glad not to be yoked.

Model City [67]

It was like walking past a store window in a fancy part of the city on which the word VERGOLDUNG has been painted in small gold block letters, and stopping to peer inside.

*

It was like realizing that you are peering into a gilding workshop, to which customers bring things to be gilded, and thinking of everything in your possession that could use a coat of gold leaf — your mood, for one.

*

It was like wanting to gild your mood or at least order a dumpster's worth of lilies to be delivered to the door of the gilding workshop, to see whether the gilders have a sense of humor.

*

It was like fantasizing about opening up a rose-painting workshop next door to the lily-gilders', so that at least the lily-gilding, rose-painting street might be a little bit honest about its beautifying lies.

Model City [68]

It was like walking through the city park after finishing work for the day and noticing that the trees have white tags tied around their trunks, and, on closer inspection, that the tags contain numbers.

*

It was like thinking about the numbered trees living arboreal life outside numbers, though the rings accumulating inside the trunks are also engaged in a form of counting.

*

It was like walking back home past the façade of a new hotel on which large white room numbers are painted under the windows, so that the travelers are turned into lab rabbits in the experiment of traveling.

*

It was like sitting back down at your desk to write an invoice for the day, grinning as you multiply the work by an hourly rate, while another ring deepens its stain inside your body.

Model City [69]

It was like feeling very uncertain one afternoon outside a non-model city, like that feeling of uncertainty one gets while riding in an elevator that opens on both sides.

*

It was like riding in an elevator feeling very uncertain, wanting the elevator to open on one side only, and to know what side before the door opens, to know that one side of the elevator is pure interior.

*

It was like thinking about the windows in the houses of the non-model city, with their ogive shapes and faulty latches, as two-way openings rendering interior life utterly porous, interior-less.

*

It was like standing inside an elevator outside a non-model city one afternoon, disturbed by the excess of apertures and openings, points of access and multiple entries — by the triumph of flow.

Model City [70]

It was like reading in a book about the model city *la cité industrielle*, in which all buildings shall be made of concrete, all corners rounded, and each bedroom shall have at least one window facing south.

*

It was like reading that *la cité industrielle* should be situated exactly between a mountain and a river, and that it should have lots of schools, but no churches or courthouses.

*

It was like thinking about the west-facing window in your own bedroom and its potential sunsets blocked by the new hotel that rose across the street, story by story, a month after you moved in.

*

It was like thinking about how *la cité industrielle* was never built, but the hotel blocking your sunsets was, how hotels will always be built, blocking sunsets, squaring corners, and placing windows facing all cardinal points.

Model City [71]

It was like lying down in a new hotel room and trying to imagine a city in which no more building is possible, a city that is already perfectly, completely, sparklingly, imperviously built.

*

It was like imagining living in that city, in which the citizens are content with the already built, in which architects do not exist, and the very word 'architect' has an old-fashioned ring to it, like 'apparatchik' or 'castellan.'

*

It was like imagining living in that city as an architect, and being unable to move to another city for sheer fascination, spending all day looking out at the perfectly built city, its perfect skyscrapers and airports and churches.

*

It was like being the architect and knowing that all cities everywhere are all already built, as he sits at his window all day, fascinated, looking out at all of it all already perfectly built.

Model City [72]

It was like traveling to a model city and staying in a hotel converted from a corset factory, wondering if the original plans for the model city had allocated any space for hotels.

*

It was like wondering if any model city anywhere had ever allocated space for any hotels, as you make love with your boyfriend in the former corset factory turned into a hotel.

*

It was like, later, combing through libraries looking at plans for model cities and finding space allocated for boot factories and poor farms, pedestrian walkways and vertical windows, but none for hotels.

*

It was like thinking about model cities and about hotels, and realizing that of course no model city ever allocated space for a hotel, for why should there be any vacancy in the fully realized ideal?

A:

Berlin and elsewhere
2010–2014

Acknowledgments

Some of these poems were published, sometimes in different versions, in the following journals: *The Chicago Review*, *Conjunctions*, *Harp and Altar*, *Molly Bloom*, *New American Writing*, *The Paris Review*, *Sentence*, *Shearsman*, *Tarpaulin Sky*, *Tupelo Quarterly*, *Vlak*, and *Zen Monster*. Three were reprinted on the Dutch translation website *Oote Oote*. I am grateful to the editors.

Some of the poems were published in German translation by Lars-Arvid Brischke in *No Man's Land* and *Karawa*; in Czech translation by Olga Pek in *Psí víno*; in Dutch translation by Hannie Rouweler in *Schoon Schip*; in Lithuanian translation by Laurynas Katkus in *Druskininkai Poetic Fall*; and in Slovak translation by Marián Andričík in *Ars Poetica*. Many thanks to the translators for their work.

I am grateful to the Corporation of Yaddo, New York; the Fundación Valparaiso, Mojacar, Spain; the International Writers and Translators Center of Rhodes, Greece; and the Helen Whiteley Center on San Juan Island, Washington State, for residencies that gave me the time and space in which to further this manuscript.

I would also like to thank the University of Georgia for a Dean's Award that allowed me to travel to Letchworth Garden City, the world's first garden city, conceived by English visionary Ebenezer Howard; and to Eisenhüttenstadt, a Socialist model city in East Germany near the border with Poland, built in

1953 as Stalinstadt (the name was changed in 1961 following the revision of Stalin's legacy after his death). The book was instigated by a visit to the model city of Anniston, Alabama. While on a residency in Greece I got to visit the Italian rationalist model city Portolago (now Lakki) on the Greek island of Leros, built during the Italian occupation. (Thanks to Valerie McGuire for getting me there.) Other model cities haunting the book include Le Corbusier's *la ville radieuse*; Tony Garnier's *la cité industrielle*; and Seaside, Florida, among others. But I was perhaps most intrigued by Berlin, object of multiple utopic and dystopic projections throughout the twentieth and twenty-first centuries.

Special thanks to Shane Anderson, Marie Borel, Lars-Arvid Brischke, Josepha Conrad, András Dörner, Camille Guthrie, Millay Hyatt, Karla Kelsey, Sarah Riggs, Julian Smith-Newman, Anthony Tognazzini, and Andrew Zawacki.

Finally, thank you to Veronika Reichl for her help in designing the cover.

Donna Stonecipher is the author of three previous books of poetry: *The Reservoir* (winner of the Contemporary Poetry Series competition, 2002); *Souvenir de Constantinople* (2007); and *The Cosmopolitan* (winner of the National Poetry Series, 2008). Her poems have been published in many journals, including *Conjunctions, New American Writing,* and *The Paris Review*, and have been translated into six languages. She lives in Berlin.

Printed in October 2024
by Rotomail Italia S.p.A., Vignate (MI) - Italy